DARKNESS TO LIGHT
WITH
HOPE

DARKNESS to LIGHT
WITH
HOPE

AN AUTOBIOGRAPHICAL SKETCH

Abraham Gold

Library of Congress Control Number: 2012911563
ISBN: Hardcover   978-1-4771-3388-0
               Softcover   978-1-4771-3387-3
               Ebook   978-1-4771-3389-7

This book was printed in the United States of America.

To order additional copies of this book, contact:

Xlibris Corporation

1-888-795-4274

www.Xlibris.com

Orders@Xlibris.com

117730

Dedicated to my children and grandchildren,
And all the young people of the world,
So they never forget.

In memory of
My parents my two sisters Sase, Sury, and two brothers
Shlomo and Martin

"MY CHILDREN MADE ME WRITE'

All these years while my children were growing up, it was too difficult for me to talk about my past. The immense terrifying madness that had erupted in history, and in the conscience of humankind was too painful As my children grew up they started to ask questions about their grandmother and grandfather. Finally I told them a little history of the war in Europe.

The Nazis in Germany set out to build a society in which there simply would be no room for the Jews. Toward the end of their reign, their goal changed; they wanted to leave behind a world in ruins in which Jews would never to have existed. The Germans everywhere in Russia, in the Ukraine, and in Lithuania, carried out the Final Solution by turning their machine guns on more than a million Jews, who were not only killed but were denied burial in a cemetery.

It is obvious that the war, which Hitler and his accomplices waged, was a war not only against Jewish men, women, and children but also against Jewish religion, Jewish culture, Jewish tradition, therefore Jewish memory. Yet having lived through this experience, I could not keep silent no matter how difficult, if not impossible, it was for me to speak. I had many things to say, I did not have the words to tell them. How was I to speak of what happened without trembling, heartbroken for all eternity, The hunger—thirst—fear—transport—selection—fire—chimney.

When it came to tell them, what did happen to their grandparents, aunts and uncles, no words came out of my mouth, we all started to cry.

In 1974, November I was given a testimonial dinner for serving as post Commander of the J.W.V. in Orangeburg New York. The editor of our town's newspaper came to our house to interview me knowing that I was a Holocaust survivor.

JWV will honor survivor of Nazi holocaust

Story and Photos

by Peter C. Bocchieri

Abe Gold, of 61 Edgewood Drive, left his family one day in July, 1944 without ever goodbye. At that point he never realized that he would never see them again.

Gold was born in Romania, one of a family of ten. In 1944 Gold was 18 years old: World War II reached him - he and his family were taken from their home by Hungarian Facists and transported by truck to the Nazi concentration camp at Auchwitz.

When Gold and his family arrived at the ominous, barbed - wire camp, they were herded off trucks, stripped of all possessions and became prisoners of the third reich.

Young children and their parents were separated from stronger youths,

Gold and his twin brother, thought they were going to work and be reunited with their family that night. But the Germans crowded little children and parents together and told them to think they were going to take showers. "The Germans ordered the people to take off their clothes," said Gold, "but instead of a shower they gave them gas, I never saw them again after that."

Eventually Gold was separated from his twin brother, which he was very close to, and was sent to work in a factory painting machinery parts. Gold worked with many German civilians. "Some of them were a hell of a nice people," said Gold.

Gold recalled the time ... a German woman was nice ... to give him a Christmas gift ... gave me a package contain... ... which I never saw before, two apples, bread

guard telling him "The sun is shining for us today, tomorrow maybe it will shine for you." The guard knew what was going to ... at that time says ...

were starving; we didn't eat for a whole week."

After regaining some strength, Gold went home to see who was left of his family. He traveled in box-

... all the way to his home town. "I remember one night falling asleep at a station. When I woke up all of the little belongings I had were gone. The robbers were stealing like mad," said Gold.

Gold found four brothers when he arrived home, but realized he couldn't stay. "I couldn't stay home," said Gold, "I was yearning for my twin brother who I later found out was still in a Nazi camp."

On his journey, Gold arrived in Austria where he found another of his brothers, but he didn't stop Gold was still searching for his twin.

"While in Austria," said Gold, "I worked KP with American GIs in order to survive. I needed money for food and shelter."

One day Gold received a letter from home informing him that his twin brother had died one week after he was liberated. "He just couldn't survive," said Gold.

Gold was ready to go to Israel but couldn't make it because of British emmigration quotas. He later found out he had an uncle in America and made the journey over. "On January ?, ? set out on the S.S. Marine Flasher, that day was my birthday."

Gold came to America all alone and worked for Alexander's Department Store. He later took a job as a tool and die maker, and lost three fingers in an accident. Six months later he entered the U.S. Army.

Gold is married now and has four children. With a lot of effort and hard work he established his own printing shop in New York City. He has been a member of the Jewish War

Veter... Post ... he ha... judge ... serve... execut... is acti... and is ...

Sout... of the ... will b... monial... Saturd...

With a family and business occupying his life, Abe Gold tries to forget the days he spent in a Nazi concentration camp in Germany where, of a family of ten, only six survived.

In the beginning, I was reluctant to speak, but soon was sharing with him memories from the time of the occupation, the dark days that marked all of us. I confided to our editor that nothing I had witnessed during that dark period had marked me as deeply as the image of cattle wagons filled with Jewish mothers, fathers, and children, at the Auschwitz train station . . . .

At that time, we knew nothing about the Nazis' extermination methods. In addition, who could have imagined such things! Seeing children torn from their parents was an outrage far beyond anything I would have thought was possible. I did tell my children everything about what happened to my parents' sisters and brothers. After that, I was not able to continue anymore. My children told me to write my story down. I promised them that soon, as I retired I would buy a computer to write my story.

In 1987, I retired and moved to the Pocono Mountains in Pennsylvania. Now I had no choice but to start writing about everything. I did buy a computer; I did promise them to write the story of myself and my family. I did not know how to begin to write my story. It did hurt me every time I started to write. I had many things to write about, but I did not have the words to write them down. Painfully aware of my limitation, I began even though my spelling became an obstacle. It became clear that it was going to take a long time to finish my story. I would pause at every sentence, and start repeatedly again.

I would come up with other verbs, other images, other silent cries. It still was not right. However, what exactly was "it"? "It" was something elusive, dark for fear of being profaned. How was I to write of them without trembling and a heart broken for all eternity? How can I describe the last journey in sealed cattle cars, the last trip toward the unknown? Or the tearing apart of entire families, entire communities.

An event that sprang from the darkest soul of man. Only those who experienced Auschwitz know what it was. Others will never know.

However, would they at least understand?

Having lived through this experience, one could not keep silent no matter how difficult, if not impossible, it was to speak. I believe those who kept silent yesterday will remain silent tomorrow. For the survivors who choose to testify, it is clear; their duty is to bear witness for the dead and for the living. They have no right to deprive future generations of a past that belongs to our collective memory.

To forget would be not only dangerous but also offensive. To forget the dead would be akin to killing them a second time. Sometimes I am asked if we knew "the response to Auschwitz"; I answer that not only we did not know it, but also that we did not even know if a tragedy of this magnitude did happened. Why there was no rebellion or demonstration:

The answer is we did not know what was going on. Moreover all the men over twenty-one to forty-five were in the army; only the young children and mothers, fathers, were at home. My first autobiography sketch consisted of sixteen pages. I wrote it while serving with the West End Ambulance as a volunteer. It was really a big undertaking and hardship.

My children were very excited; they encouraged me to write from the beginning off my life. In 1998, we moved to West Palm Beach, Florida, that's when I began, writing my story.in earnest.

It took me four years to finish my autobiographical sketch. It consisted of 44 pages. Now I was searching for someone to edit my book. In 2002, I met Dr. Robert Shostak, professor of English-Education, who brought my life story to publication. I printed one hundred books.

PREFACE

I hope that what I have written here will help to remind both old and young alike that the freedom we enjoy in our great land should never be taken for granted. It is my wish that this story depicting the fate of the my entire family, trapped in the horror of the Nazi regime of the late 1930's and describing their suffering at the hands of the brutal Romanian Iron Guard, the Hungarian gendarme, and the bestial followers of Hungary's Arrow Cross Party is never repeated in the history of mankind.

To prevent the reader from being confused by the change in my last name, let me explain.

My father Jacob Preisler married my mother Blanca Gold in a Jewish ceremony and no record of the marriage was ever recorded with civil authorities. When my mother tried to enroll my twin brother and me in public school, the authorities could find no proof of her marriage to my father and so whoever was in charge decided she was not really married. After talking it over, my father and mother thought that to avoid trouble with the authorities, from that time on, they would use my mother's last name, Gold. I believe we also felt Gold sounded better and we would less likely be the objects of anti-Semitism.

THE LIGHT YEARS

LIGHT

On January 7, 1926, twin boys were born to Jacob Preisler and his wife Blanca (Gold) Preisler. The twins caused a big commotion in the small village of Strimba located in the Carpathian Mountains of Transylvania in Romania. The villagers could not believe that twins could be born to a mother who had already given birth to eight other children. Therefore, there was a great celebration to welcome the latest edition to the Preisler family, my brother Martin and me. Because we were identical twins, my. mother pierced my left ear and my brother's right ear so that my mother could tell us apart. They told us later on that, the piercing was also part of a superstition that no harm would come to us as a result.

After World War 1, the Romanians occupied Transylvania, which had previously belonged to Hungary. In our little village of Strimba, the Romanians and Hungarians lived harmoniously with one another, and somewhat less enthusiastically, with the Jews who lived in their own section of the village. However, there existed a peaceful co-existence based on tolerance and limited respect for each other, our religious institutions, social organization, and tradition.

Our village was not unlike the numerous small communities throughout Europe. There was the obvious division between Jews and Gentiles, but the situation was accepted with a shrug by most, and people got on with their lives. Life was not a very easy one by today's standards. We had no indoor plumbing or central heating.

The winters were cold with temperatures frequently, below freezing. Although life was not easy, my childhood was lots of fun. My family may have been disadvantaged in many ways, but I was too happy to realize it. As I grew older, my life began to change. Around four o'clock every morning, my father and sometimes my older brother, would be up to make a fire in the wood stove that supplied meager heat to the house. We also started a fire in the kitchen stove so my mother could prepare breakfast.

Mother's work seemed endless. Right after breakfast, she began to prepare the noon meal. Then she tackled the laundry and other housework. She never knew the joy of high-tech housekeeping; but like to think she was happy in those precious days when we were all together, in spite of the chores we loaded on her dear shoulders.

My father who was well educated in Hebrew and Jewish law worked as a teacher in a Hebrew school in the winter. In the summer, he was able to get a job in a hotel where he supervised the food preparation to make certain, the food was kosher. We lived in a brick house with a big backyard where we planted a garden, kept two cows and raised some chickens and geese. We were able to grow enough vegetables to take care of most of our needs, and the chickens and geese provided us with eggs and meat.

Each morning I remember watching the herders walk through town blowing their horns to gather the livestock for pasturing across the river. Each evening the procession returned and the animals knew where they belonged to and returned to their owners.

We also had a large bam with an oven, used only for Passover to bake matzos for the whole village. The village consisted of twenty Jewish families, most of them volunteered. The rest of the village, were Christian people.

The month before Passover, we started our preparation, for backing the matzos. We needed to hire some men and women to help us, but many people in the village worked as volunteers.

One day in July 1929, I remember an overcast sky and a chilly breeze. Soon the rain came and it continued for days. Our village was flooded, and our house and bam destroyed. We had lost everything. My father had to decide whether to stay and rebuild—or to leave. My oldest brother Shlomo left to attend a Yeshiva, a Hebrew parochial school and my brother Leon went to Bucharest, the capital of Romania. He went there for a job, he was promised

My older sister Sosa and two other brothers, Willy, and Philip, went to stay with an aunt in Cluj, which was the capital of Transilvania. The Hungarians called it Kolozvar. The only ones left at home were my sister Sury and three brothers, Sulem, Alex, Martin and me.My fathers decided to move the family to a large town. We bought two horses and a big wagon, and packed it up with what we had saved from the flood. Our journey began with five children and my parents. Our first stop was in Reteag, a small village where our aunt and uncle lived, and we stayed with them for the night. The next stop was the town of Dej. We had some relatives there and my father decided that he would try to make a future for our family in that town.

In 1930, we rented a house and lived there for about a year. My father found that he could not make a living and the schools were not very good. Since my older brothers and sister were learning a trade in Cluj and my twin brother and I would soon need a Hebrew school, my father thought that he might try his luck in Cluj.

It was 1931, when we moved to Cluj. Because we had such a large family, the best place we could find to live was a large basement apartment with a big backyard. Our property owner was Hungarian, and she gave each of us a Hungarian name. My twin brother's name was Marcy, and my name was Jeno. Most of the tenants were Hungarians and Jews, so we learned to speak Hungarian. Until then, we had spoken only Yiddish and Romanian.

Sury and Alex went to public school. My other sister Sose had a job as a nanny, my brother Solomon was a carpenter, Willie and Fulop were tailors. My father still had a hard time getting a steady job. Sometimes he would get work in the hotel across the street from where we lived. He worked in catering helping to supervise the preparation of food to make sure it was kosher. In 1932, our parents were anxious to send my brother and me to a Jewish school, but the Jewish school was private and they did not have the money for tuition. Someone at the hotel where my father worked offered to help and he was able to enroll us in school.

The following year in September 1933, my twin brother and I started the private school, which ran from eight-thirty in the morning to twelve-thirty in the afternoon.

After school, we went to a day-care center for orphans and poor children for lunch. While we were there, we helped to set the tables and served lunch to the local preschool children. In the afternoon, we went to Hebrew school from two to five o'clock.

In 1934, my sister Sose got married.

They moved out, but our basement apartment was no longer large enough for our growing family. By growing the children became taller and more mature, and in stature. Therefore, my parents began to look for another place to live, but apartments large enough for our big family were hard to find. My father thought it would be a good idea to build our own house. He even found an acre of land that would be very suitable to build a house, but he did not have enough money to buy it.

At the same time, two nephews of my father were looking for a piece of land on which they could build a house. My father had saved some money; it was not enough to buy the land, he had a brother in the United States, who sent my father some money, so he asked his nephews if they would want to buy the acre of land with him. They all agreed that this would be a good idea. They bought the acre of land, on the outskirts of the little village called Somesan, about five miles outskirts of the City.

As soon as the final papers were signed, my father began to prepare the land for our house. My older brother Sulem made up molds for making bricks. We bought yellow clay and straw and mixed it up to make the bricks. It was a tough job. It was fun in the beginning but after two weeks, it was not fun anymore. Only three of us did the work, Sulem my twin brother and me. The rest of the brothers helped occasionally. But by the fall, we had finished, making the bricks.

In the spring 1935, we started to build. The house consisted of a large kitchen and bedroom and a small room for the groceries and vegetables. We had to get additional help so we could move in before school started. Although the house was ready inside, it was not finished on the outside. Ready or not we moved in anyway. There was no plumbing or electricity.

We used kerosene lamps for light. We had a well to draw water for household cleaning and garden. For drinking water we used a pump on the comer of the street where everybody in the neighborhood came to get water.

In the kitchen, we had a large build-in wood burning stove. That was the best place to sleep because the bedroom had no stove.

We made it comfortable in the bedroom by heating a brick on the stove before we went to sleep and putting it at the bottom of the bed to keep our feet warm. The sleeping arrangement was very cozy. My father slept on a cot, and my mother and Sury slept together in a large bed. My twin brother, Alex and I slept in another bed, and my other three brothers slept in the kitchen where we had two large benches and a cot. The bathroom was outside the house; and in the winter, it was too cold to go out, so we used little potties inside

For recreation, we created our own fun. We always invited friends to our home on the weekends. We usually played soccer, or went to a small stream to fish and swim. When Purim came it was like Halloween (Purim is a Jewish holiday that commemorates the deliverance of the deliverance of the Jewish people in the an ancient Persia Empire from destruction in the wake of a plot by Haman, a story recorded in the Biblical Book of Queen Ester Our mother baked a lot of cakes, on this holiday because the custom was to exchange cakes with our neighbors. It took us all morning to make deliveries.

The neighbors sent their children with their cake. In the afternoon, we got dressed up in funny clothes and went to the city to perform the verses we made up to get extra treats. Sometimes we even made some money, but we did not do any tricks. Before the Passover holiday, the town was busy baking matzos. They were stored in a warehouse, and one week before the holiday began, they were, distributed to every family, according to the size. My brother and I would help deliver the matzos, and we would make enough money to buy clothes for the holiday. The clothes were old suits we purchased at a flea market.

In about the same time, the houses of our two cousins were finished and they moved in. Not far from our house, six other Jewish families lived. This made it very good for us, because we had enough adults to have our own minyan. Therefore, in the event of bad weather, we did not have to walk an hour and fifteen minute, to the synagogue in the city. We had service at neighbor's house, which was larger than ours. When school started, we had to walk more than one hour to get there. The walk was not that bad except in the winter, when it took us much longer, because of the snow and ice. We also did not like the days when it got dark early, and for about five miles, there were no streetlights.

When we got to that part of our walk, my brother and I always waited for a wagon or an adult to follow home. My father and my brother Sulem had a hard time getting a job so they bought horse and wagon and went into the business of buying and selling livestock. They went to nearby villages to purchase livestock. Then on Thursday and Friday, they went to the market to sell their merchandise. On Fridays, we had only morning classes, and in the afternoon, there was no religious school, so my twin brother and I went to the market to help with deliveries so we could make some money.

After the deliveries on Friday, we always went to the ritual bath, (Mikva) to prepare for the Sabbath. Then we went right home to change our clothes and get ready for the Sabbath meal. My mother would also wear clean clothes and place a kerchief on her head as she lit the Shabbat candles, and said prayers for our well-being. Friday night was the only time we all sat together to eat a meal. We sang Shabbat melodies, and always had a good time as a family. On Saturday morning, my father my twin brother and I went to the Synagogue.

Being Jewish, however, was not always so easy. For example, on our way home from Hebrew school, which ended at five o'clock, a small group of Hungarian gentile kids would confront us and call us unpleasant names. We just ignored them and walked away, but that did not last for long. Soon they started to throw stones at us and tried to pick a fight. One day my brother and I decided, we had had enough, and confronted them.

After giving our tormentors a good beating, they did not bother us again. Also at this time, the political situation began to get worse. The Iron Guard party in Romania was both anti-Semitic, and anti-government. They were inspired by the Nazis, to increase their activities against the Jews.

THE BEGINNING OF DARK

DARK

In 1937, a few miles from the border not far from where we lived, clashes were increasing between the Romanian army and the forces of the Hungarian military and the so-called "Free Bands." The Hungarians were trying to bully the Romanians back into the old alliance.

At the same time, it was a signal had been given to the Hungarians in our hometown, to begin their own anti-Semitic activities. Attitudes changed overnight. Some of my friends would not look at us, pretending they did not know us. Others, in opposition to the growing anti-Jewish sentiment, still recognized us as their neighbors and friends. Hungarian Jews would arrive in Cluj and tell us about the hard times they were having in Hungary.

Not only the adults were scorned openly because they were Jews, but the campaign was actually reaching children. A ruling by the Hungarian government, for example, decreed that only one out of every ten Jewish students was permitted to attend a university.

News from Germany of atrocities committed against Jewish communities began arriving with sickening, and alarming regularity. Synagogues where being burned, businesses looted, people being carted off to labor camps, all while the Nazis kept up a steady drum roll of propaganda against the Jews, in Germany and everywhere else.

In 1938, it was not the right historical moment for the Jews of Europe to expect any influential nation to champion their cause and save them from near-extinction. Therefore, the stage was set world conditions were ideal, for the most massive brutalization of an entire ethnic group whose only wish was to be good citizens of the countries of their birth or adoption. Most of those who wanted to leave Germany and the other countries where, they felt threatened were too poor to move. A few could afford to escape to Switzerland or other neutral countries, like China, but the doors of most western nations, including the United States, were shut tight. The greatest blow of all was Britain's refusal to allow long-promised emigration to Palestine.

They who wanted to emigrate to Palestine could not because the British were steadfast in their policy stop the influx of immigrants, going so far as to sink a Greek ship bringing the refugees and heartlessly allowing Jewish men women and children to drown within sight of Palestine. Survivors of this particular incident were sent to an International camp on Cyprus, the Mediterranean island.

This, in spite of the Balfour Declaration issued in World War I. which stated, clearly "His Majesty's Government view with favor the establishment in Palestine of a national home for the Jewish people, and will use their best endeavors to facilitate the achievement of this objective . . ."

We knew the Hungarians were up to something when they began to mobilize on the Romanian border. The Romanians wishing to avoid a bloody fight, agreed to return the State of Transylvania to Hungary. In August, of 1938, shock waves began to ripple through our lives. After enjoying the relative freedom off being a Jew in Romania for twenty years, we were now occupied by a new Hungarian dictatorial regime. The Arrow Cross Guard carried out the policies of this new regime.

They built a new headquarters on the outskirts of our town, and began their campaign against the Jews. They put up a large sign that read, "Jew go and save your homeland", and began to distribute propaganda literature all over the town. The Hungarian regime gave a new decree that boys from the age of twelve had to serve once a week as a boy scout (Levente) for the military. In addition, Jewish kids had to wear a yellow ribbon on their clothing and were forced to work at a new ski slope for six hours a week.

From the beginning of the occupation, the murderous behavior of some ofthe Arrow Cross Guards were despised by most of the Hungarian population, even by many of the more radical citizens of Kolosvar. (Cluj) Soon my brother and I began to encounter new problems on our way home from school. The same Hungarian kids, who used to start fights with us, now would send younger kids to try to start a fight and call us names. We were smart enough to ignore them, and to take another longer, but safer, route to school.

In January 1939, my brother and I celebrated our 13ᵗʰ birthday (Bar Mitzvah) at the house of our neighbor. They had a large house and there was a (Kiddush) which means celebration honor of our 13th birthday, (Bar

Mitzvah) is a way of coming into our religion as a man, and no longer a child. He alone is responsible for his deeds. Hi is included in the special services of the temple. That was the first time we wore a new suit. Actually, they were old suits turned inside out so they just looked new; my brother Fulop did the alterations.

Action and attitudes in town began to take on frightening forms. The faces of the town's people reflected fear of the future. Everything was happening too quickly. The entire continent seemed to be erupting around us wherever Jews lived.

We never dreamed that what would happen would horrify and disgust the entire planet. Reports of anti-Semitism and brutality were beginning to mount. Verbal insults and physical assaults were commonplace. The Hungarian Arrow Cross Party was making day-to-day living a terror-filled ordeal for Jews in Kolosvar. (Cluj)

The situation worsened as Jews began to stream across the border from Poland. A few financially well off poles used Kolosvar (Cluj) as a rest stop on their way to friendly countries. In the meantime, my mother was working hard to help make ends meet. Along with her daily chores, she would go to the nearby airport where she picked up-laundry from the Jewish soldiers who wore civilian clothes with yellow armbands that were used to identify them.

My sister Sury helped my mother with all the work she had to do, plus she got a job as a bookkeeper. My brother Alex was able to get work, fixing bicycles and sewing machines, As little we had, there was always enough food to invite two soldiers for a Shabbat dinner.

Martin and I continued to go to school. It was becoming harder every day, and unbearable for us to see our father and mother struggling so hard to provide for us.

In June 1940, there was a conference in Budapest, Hungary of all Jewish organization; the conference lasted five days, ending on a hopeful note. They sent letters to various influential groups within the western world, particularly the United States and Britain, in hopes those nations would take some action to save off the impending crisis for European Jewry.

We waited for months for action that never came. It seemed to us our Jewish people in the western countries were interested only in themselves.

The situation was getting worse and worse. It was becoming more and more for my parents to provide for us, so we left public and Hebrew school and where admitted to a boarding school were we could learn a trade.

The school was for poor children and orphans, who lived in rural areas, and did not have the funds to send their children to learn a trade. They took in children who were able to pay, to learn a trade.

The photograph of the boys at the apprentice school was taken
six months before my brother and me were admitted.

Martin became an apprentice to be a cabinetmaker and I chose to be a lithographer. Before I was accepted, I took a test that I found to be not difficult and passed it with high marks. Martin did not take a test. Living in a boarding school of apprentices was not easy it was almost like living in a military academy. We had a list of duties to be done every day. Wake up time was six o'clock in the morning, except on weekends and holidays.

We had to make up our beds and be ready by seven o'clock for breakfast. The hardest job we had was to cut wood and this we had to do once a week. The only good thing about this hard job was that the younger kids could cut wood for the older boys for money. This helped my brother and me because in the first year, our salary went to the school and they only gave us a small allowance, after the first year; they increased both our salary and allowance.

Some of the boys where from rural areas and wanted to learn a trade, they all started from age of 14, we also increased, our academic schooling. All the boys wore a different cap and clothes. In 1942, my brother Sulem was drafted into the army and that was very hard on my father, because

Sulem was a big help to him. A few months later, both Willie and Fulop were also drafted. My parent's hearts were broken: Alex left for Budapest, my brother and me were at the school of apprentice, and Sury was the only one left at home. Life returned normal. Every night we would listen to the London radio. They announced encouraging news about the daily bombing of Germany, the preparation of the Second Front. In addition, we, the Jews of Kolosvar, waited for better days that surely were soon to come. My mother was beginning to think it was high time to find an appropriate match for Sury. ——— *hoped* ——————→ ↙

The year 1943.passed

In spring 1944 there was splendid news from the Russian front. There could no longer be any doubt: Germany would be defeated. It was only matter of time, months or weeks, perhaps. The trees were in bloom. It was a year like so many others, with its spring, its engagements, its weddings, its births. The people were saying," The Red Army is advancing with giant strides . . . Hitler will not be able to harm us, even if he wants to . . ." Yes, even we doubted his resolve, to exterminate us. Wipe out an entire population dispersed throughout so many nations? In the middle of the twentieth century?

Budapest radio announced that the Fascist party had seized power. The regent Horthy Miklos was forced to ask a leader of the pro-Nazi Nyilas party to form a new government. Yet we still were not worried. Of course, we had heard of the Fascists, but it was all in the abstract. It meant nothing more to us than a change of ministry. The next day brought more news: German troops had penetrated Hungarian territory with the government's approval.

Finally, people began to worry in earnest. The brother of our caretaker returned from the capital for Passover and told us. "The Jews of Budapest live in an atmosphere of fear terror and anti-Semitic acts take place every day, in the streets, in the trains. The Fascists attack Jews stores, synagogues. The situation is becoming very serious . . ."

The news spread though Kolosvar like wildfire, and soon it was all people talked about. But not for long in less than three days, German Army vehicles made an appearance on our streets. The Fascists were already in power, the verdict was already out.

On the seventh day of Passover, the curtain finally rose; the Germans arrested the leaders of the Jewish community. The race toward death had begun. A few days later a new orders were given: All Jews were to wear a yellow star on their clothes and lapel. People who changed their religion had to wear a white ribbon on their arm.

It was a frightening and horrifying ordeal and fewer and fewer people went out on the streets. They were afraid to go to work, especially the people who were religious and had to go the synagogue. Every day new acts of brutality were out against Jewish people it became very frightening not knowing who would be the next victim. Stores were broken into and looted. In order to go to the city to make a little money, my father had to cut off his beard. People were just afraid to go out on the street. My brother and I went to work folding over our lapels to hide the star. We were able to get away with it because our work clothes hid our true identities.

We were able to visit our parents twice a month and bring them some groceries and other necessities. Every male over age twenty-one, had to go in to the army. My boss and the supervisor and the rest of the males were also called in to the army. I was the only male left in the shop. I felt very proud that I was able to manage the shop myself, but that did not last long. Every other day there were new restrictions were announced. Jews where not permitted out on the street from five o'clock in the evening to seven o'clock in the morning.

Ultimately, our printing shop closed so the rest of the boys did not go to work anymore. We were told our School would close soon. Our professor told us to call our parents about the school closing. We contacted our parents, and told them that we were coming home soon for good.

All of us were very sad to leave, not knowing when we would be seeing each other again. We all got two blankets to take home, and some food to take home. Our Professor told us the ones who eat onions with our meals would be healthier and withstand all the work that will be ahead of us. I never forgot his advice and I still eat onions whenever I had a chance.

When we arrived home, we were surprised to see our older sister and her two children, as well as our sister Sury, living with my mother and father. Soon after returning home, my father told us, his voice breaking, there were rumors that the German government needed all the young men and woman to work in Germany. Grandparents would take care of the very young. The young adults would be working in factories. It seems that here we are too close to the front" he said . . .

Next, new orders where issued for all Jews. We were permitted to leave the house for only two hours from nine to eleven in the morning. Two days later, Hungarian police came to our house and told us to get ready to leave. My brother and I, made pants out of blankets for the winter. We were told to pack clothes for both summer and winter, but not to pack more than we could carry in our hands. The next day a large truck pulled up and two armed soldiers came into our house, and told us to take our belongings. We were ready. I went out first. I did not look at my parents' faces. I did not want to break into tears. I looked at my house in which I had spent years. Yet I felt little sadness. My mind was empty.

My father was crying. It was the first time I saw him cry. I had never thought it possible. As for my mother, she was walking, her face a mask, without a word, deep in thought. My brother and I helped put the belongings in the truck. Then we all climbed into the truck; my older sister and her two children; my mother, father, my young sister Sury who was engaged, to be married in two months; and my twin brother Martin and me. They also picked up my two cousins and their families.

After two hours, we finally arrived at our destination. Taking our bundles, we dropped them to the ground: We all prayed, "Oh God, Master of the Universe, in your infinite compassion, have mercy on us." They took us to a large brick factory, where all the Jewish people were gathered I had never seen so many people in one place before. In our town there were approximately 20,000 Jews. Every day more people arrived we did not know how long we were going to be there, but thank God it was not too long.

We had to sleep on the floor for about three days with only a blanket separating us from the cold cement. The few days we spent here went by with everyone calm.

People got along rather well. There was no longer any distinction, between rich and poor, notables and others: We were all people condemned to the same fate which was still unknown. There were those who said, "Who knows, they may be sending us away for our own good. The front is getting closer; we shall soon hear the guns.

They treated us like cattle and dogs. What we endured, in those three days, left us with an unforgettable and painful memory. They made up groups; we were the third group to leave, We had no idea where we were going. We walked for almost two hours to the other side of the town, where I knew there was a railroad station. It was terrible to see how difficult it was for the old, and sick, and for parents with small children, who struggled to make the long trip to the railroad station. During the long walk, many were ill. It was like a big holiday for the town's people. Many of them lined up, to watch us as we walked. Some of the folks cheered, some of them cried and some remained silent

The people who were ill, they were taken away, never to be seen again. It was the longest and most painful journey, not knowing where they are taking us. We finally arrived at the railroad station, where a convoy of cattle cars was waiting. I could see the look of horror and fright on faces of every one. The tracks were lined up with empty cattle wagons The Hungarian police made us climb into the cars. They placed seventy or eighty persons in each car handing us bread, a few pails of water. They checked the bars on the windows to make sure they would not come loose. One person was in charge of every car: We still did not know where they were taking us, which were very upsetting to everyone.

When we finished boarding, they closed the wagon doors. The only light we had come from the two small windows on each side of the wagon. There was little air.

A prolonged whistle pierced the air. The wheels began to grind and we were on our way. There were many children crying. The lucky ones found themselves near a window. After two days of travel, thirst became intolerable, as did the heat. There was still some food left. But we never ate enough to satisfy our hunger. Our strategy was to economize, to save for tomorrow. Tomorrow could be worse yet. When the train stopped in a small town on the Czechoslovakian border, we realized we were not staying in Hungary. The door of the car slid aside. A German officer stepped in accompanied by a Hungarian lieutenant, acting as his interpreter. "From this moment on, you are under the authority of the German Army. Anyone who owns gold, silver, or watches must hand them over now. Anyone who keeps any of these items is going to be punished on the spot. Secondly, anyone who is ill should report to the hospital car that is all."

The Hungarian lieutenant moved around with a basket and retrieved the last possessions from those who chose not to go on tasting the bitterness of fear. I could see that some of the families had run out of food, and some had too much food, but they would not share it with anybody else, because they did not know how long the trip was going to be. They could know that: we were only about three hours away from our final destination. The conditions were good. We were told that, families would not be separated. Only the young, would work in the factories. The old and the sick would find work in the fields. Confidence soared. Suddenly we felt free of previous nights' of terror.

We gave thanks to God. Around eleven o'clock, the train started moving again. The convoy was rolling slowly. A quarter of an hour later, it began to slow down even more. Through the window, we saw barbed wire. We understood that this was the camp. It must have been around midnight, when the doors opened. German SS swarmed all over yelling. "Ales heraus! Mach shnell." {Everyone out! Hurry up} they told us to leave everything in the train, including the little food we had.

We all jumped out. I helped my mother and father, and many other elderly folks.

Mothers Fathers Sisters and Brothers from Hungary. On the unloading ramp front of the Concentration Camp KL Auschwitz 11—Birkenau.

There were many sick people some with heart trouble diabetic, and other ailments and some of them were near death. The sick people were taken away with the stretchers. I remember the place was all lit up, and everyone was frightened when we saw the big wire fences all around us. I could see this big iron gate and above it a sign that read, "Albeit Macht Frei" (Work Makes You free)

Oswiecin II (kl. Auschwitz) Main gate

They walked everyone through the gate into the camp, which I learned was called Auschwitz, and we had no idea what was going to happen. Now we did realized that what we left in the wagons we will not see again. It tortures me to remember what happened next. The SS came toward us wielding a club. He commanded: "Men to the left, women to the right"

They did not separate, the children from their mothers. There was no time to think, to give them a hug or a kiss, or say good bye to my mother and my two sisters and nephews. My brother and I already felt my fathers hand press against mine; we were all alone. In a fraction of a second, I could see my mother, my sisters, and two nephews, moved to the right. I watched them walk further and further away.

There were polish capos who spoke Yiddish, German and Polish told us to cooperate as much as possible. We asked them what was going to happen; they did not tell us anything, the only thing they told us was to make sure that the elderly folks took care of the children. My sister Sosa, and her children, had a very rough time. To help my sister, Sury did hold on to one of her nephew's hand.

It was very hard and sickening to see all the grandparents, parents and children crying. We just did not know what was going to happen to all of us. "We mustn't give up hope, even now as the sword hangs over our heads. So taught our sages . . ." Every few yards, there stood an SS man, his machine gun trained on us.

As we passed in front of a high-ranking German SS officer, he pointed his finger to show who should go to left or right. Only my brother and

I went to the left. My father went to the right. We were not able to say anything; not even a goodbye or give him a hug. At that moment we did not know if we were going to see him again.

Later, we found out that the older people and mothers with young children were gassed. We just could not believe what was happening. Because my younger sister was holding one of her nephews by the hand, the SS officer must have thought that she was the mother and that is why they did not separate my younger sister from the boy, directing her to the same line where my mother and the rest of the family went. Now there was only my brother and me, we hugged each other and cried. All the males were taken to barracks where we stayed for the night. Next to us, were barracks filled with gypsies.

I was very surprised to see them there knowing they had been taken away prior to 1944, to perform hard labor. The SS asked us if we had any gold hidden in our shoes or clothes. They said that if we told the truth, we would not be punished. We were scared and frightened and revealed that we had some gold. They threatened us that they would have to search each person separately. After that, the SS ordered us to take off our clothes and shoes, and they cut our hair and take a shower . . .

After that, the SS gave us clothes with stripes, just like common prisoners. They made us wear metal tags around our necks and they also sewed numbers on our clothes. My number was 49119. We returned to our barracks, not knowing at the time what was happening to our parents, two sisters, and two nephews. The people who were there before we came were Polish Jews. The Germans made them overseers, over the other prisoners. They were called (Capos) and they knew everything what was going on in the camp.

They told us what happened to everyone who went to the right. Later of course, we learned that they also had to remove their clothes, have their haircut, and take a shower. But instead of water shower, they were all gassed to death. It was shocking and frightening to know that we would never see our parents or sisters any more. We just stood and our tears were running down our cheeks. Our thoughts were with the rest of our brothers.

Suddenly, silence became more oppressive. An SS officer had come in and, along with him the smell of the Angel of Death.

He arranged us in the center of the barrack and spoke. You are in a concentration camp in Auschwitz. In addition, Auschwitz is not a convalescent home it is a concentration camp. Here you must work. If you work, you will live: if not you will be going straight to the crematorium, work or crematorium-the choice is yours."

We had already lived through a lot that night. We thought that nothing could frighten us anymore. However, his harsh words sent shivers through us. The food we got was just enough to live on. In the morning we had black coffee, for lunch potato soup, and for supper some other soup and a loaf of bread, which we had to carry around with us all day, because there were no lockers. More and more people arrived every day. Later a High German officer asked all specialists—and machinists to step forward!"

My brother Martin told them he was a cabinetmaker and I was a printer and worked a printing press. The German officer asked all specialists and machinists, as I was working with a printing press; to me it was a machine. I raised my hand, not knowing that they would separate each occupation. Next day they gathered us all together and took our names and tag numbers. They also took the names of the professions of the rest of the men who were there. My brother registered as a cabinetmaker.

From Left My brother Martin and me.   My Sister Sury

The pictures where taken in 1943; I have gotten them from my brother Fulop. All my pictures were lost in Auschwitz.

The following day we all had to line up and they called us out by our numbers. They divided us into three groups, and my brother and I were put in different groups. At the time, I did not know that we were going to be separated.

They took the machinists, and loaded us into trucks and took us to the railroad station. We got off the trucks, lined up, and were counted. After two hours of waiting, they gave us some food, and walked us across the railroad yard and loaded us into cattle wagons.

Each wagon had an SS guard and I felt that everything was happening so fast that I could not think. Then I realized with deep sadness that they had separated me from my twin brother and I did not know when we would see each other again.

The train started, to roll after sitting for about two hours, someone who spoke German, asked the SS guard to let us stand up. He yelled at us, not to speak to him in German because it sounded Jewish. He wanted us to speak to him in the language of Ukraine. Luckily, somebody spoke Russian and he asked if we could stand and he agreed. We found out later that, the SS guard could not speak German. After a few hours, we arrived at a small camp with barbed wire, lights, and the same slogan over the camp's entrance gate, "Albeit macht Frei." Some people had already arrived at the camp when we got there. I soon learned it was a slave labor camp. The name of the camp was Bad Warmbrun, it was near Hirshburg. The camp had a single building, and twelve barracks. Each barrack had eight rooms, with twelve bunk beds in each room, twenty four of us slept in one room.

Here to each barracks had an overseer called, Capo. They were Polish Jews who were in camp. They all spoke the German language well. We got up at five o'clock and the Capo showed us how to make our beds which consisted of two blankets one was over the straw the other to cover our self. If you did not make your bed the right way, you would be punished. In the winter when it was very cold, we doubled up to keep warm. For our daily rations, we were provided a loaf of bread. The bread was then divided in three pieces. A big fight broke out about who was going to get the middle or the end of the portion? Our group had a scale. It was a piece of wood with two strings on each end and one in the middle.

The fight did not stop, on day the Capo came and did see what was going on, and it just happened that I was doing the measuring. The other two kids and I were puniest. Each one of us got three lashes on our backs, after that the bread was cut and the Capo was the one who did give each one their portion. We had to carry bread around with us all day because there were no lockers. Those who work in the factory, were given two cigarettes. For breakfast we had a cup of coffee for lunch potato soup, and for supper potato and barley soup.

The food we got was just enough to live on. After breakfast, they counted us and picked about five hundred of us to work at a large factory. The factory was within walking distance, and when we got there they counted us again. They divided us into groups, and each group worked in a different part of the factory. They assigned me to operate a large drill press. The supervisor asked me if I could handle the drill which looked very easy to me; my answer was yes.

Some of the men were assigned to work outside the factory. They placed these men six to a group with one SS guard who stayed with them all day. For lunch, they counted us again and also after leaving the factory. After a day's work, these men were very tired. Those of us who worked inside the factory were lucky. We had no guards, only a civilian supervisor.

That man did not speak Yiddish and spoke only Hungarian and it was very bad because the Capos only spoke Polish, German and Yiddish. One month later, the bad conditions started to affect a lot of us and some of the men became very weak and got sick. Each day we lost more and more people, and I was very heart broken because I knew I would not see my friends anymore. One day, I heard two brothers whispering to each other. We must do something. We cannot let them kill us: One was muttering: "Let us escape . . ." Let the world learn about the existence of Auschwitz.

A few days later, the brothers did escape. They took their blankets, threw them over the electric wire, and escaped. We all wished them the best of luck.

The next morning we felt the tension, and anguish on every one of their faces, as we were lined up for the Appel in the Appelplatz, surrounded by electrified barbed wire, to count us, They had discovered the two brothers were missing. we stood there for about an hour ; they told us if we tried to escape we would all suffer

One of the saddest days in camp when we learned they had found the brothers. After searching for three days they were captured and brought back to the camp. On Saturday as we returned from work, we saw two gallows, erected on the Appel platz, the following morning. They had all of us line up in front of the gallows. The SS surrounding us, machine guns aimed.

They made us stand for a few hours, then the SS (Obersharp Fuhrer) head of the camp, read the verdict. The two brothers were brought out in chains and made to step onto chairs. In unison, the nooses were placed around their necks. All eyes were on the two brothers. At the signal, the two chairs were tripped over and the brothers were hanged right before our eyes.

There was total silence in the camp. Then they told us and warned what would happen if we tried to escape. After that, we all returned to our barracks in shock and tried to comfort each other as we were weeping . . . We all recited the mourners (Kadish.) It is a prayer for the memory of the dead.

As the days went by, more people arrived from Czechoslovakia. They were the replacements for those who were no longer with us.

The summer was coming to an end. Soon the High Holidays, Rosh Hashanah, the Jewish New Year, came upon us. It was a holiday without rejoicing, a holiday with tears. We had some services and we prayed: "Sh'ma koleynu adonai eloheynu hus v'rachehm aleynu." (Hear our voice, O Lord our G-D, spare us and have compassion upon us.) All of us cried and sang. Anima-amin be-emunah sh'leima b'viat ha-mashiach V'af alpi sh' yitma-mey-ha im kol ze ani mamin chakeh lo b'chi yom sheyavo. (I believe with perfect faith in the coming of the Messiah, and although he may tarry. I will wait daily for his coming.) The service ended with Kadish. Each of us recited Kadish for his parents, brothers, sisters, and ourselves.

When Yom Kippur the Day of Atonement came, we wondered should we fast? To fast could mean more rapid death. In this place, we were always fasting. It was Yom Kippur year-round. Some did fast we needed to show God that even in hell, we were capable of singing His praises. Although they counted us each morning, every other Friday, we had a special "Appel" or roll call and that was the most frightening for all of us. We had to line up for more than an hour even when it rained or was bitter cold. A German general would show up and randomly, pick individuals who looked sick or weak. They told us these people were sent for what they called "Wieder erholing" Rest and recuperation.

This procedure was very frightening for all of us because we never saw those people again, and we never knew who was going to be next. I cannot imagine how each of us prayed and hoped not to be selected. After about three months, things began going downhill very fast. Some of the young boys in my barracks did not feel well enough to work. They remained in the barracks and in addition, they were too weak to move and soon they died in their bunks. The only day off we had, was Sunday, and in that day we had to clean ourselves, and each month we pick up clean clothes. On Sunday, I used to volunteer in the kitchen to peel potatoes. I would manage to sneak out some potato peelings, which I shared with the boys in my room. We cooked the potato peelings in a tin can; we had a picnic eating. One day they caught me, and I had to skip a couple of Sunday's, but then we started our little plan allover again.

Each morning on our way to work, we would check in the bins where the scrap metal was collected. Once or twice, a week, we would find hidden there a small package containing: two potatoes, and two carrots. Later we learned that several German women who worked the night shift left the food there whenever they could. One day a kid hid his daily ration of bread in a closet where he worked.

The Gestapo guard who walked the isle and watched us work, noticed that the kid took something out of the closet. The next day the Gestapo arrested the German supervisor and accused him of giving bread to the kid. We never saw him again, later we found out that the supervisor had committed suicide.

As conditions became worse and worse, we did not know what would become of us or how much more we could take. However, the few who still had the will to live tried not to think about tomorrow. We thought only about how to get through each day

Early in December, I was in an accident when my hand caught, in the gear of a machine. A woman helped me by giving me first aid. Soon after the factory had finished most of its work, they transferred me to the paint shop to paint the parts that we already finished.

When I got there, my boss an elderly woman, asked me my name and nationality, and wanted to know what crime I had committed: I simple told her that, "Ich bin ein Jude," I am a Jew, and that was my crime.

Just before Christmas, the same woman approached me and told me that there was a small package for the holiday hidden in a scrap metal bin. She was afraid to give it to me herself. The package contained an apple, two cooked potatoes, two carrots, some sugar, and bread.

The following week, two days before Christmas, another German woman gave me a package and pleaded with me not to tell the other woman, what she had done. I told her in German not to be afraid because the other woman had already given me a package. She told me that she knew the other woman is very nice, but she was too frightened to let anyone know what she had done. Therefore I thanked her and promised not to tell anyone anything. Now I knew for sure that the Germans, themselves were afraid of each other.

Because I was so hungry, I ate everything in the first package by myself. The second package I shared with my friends. Some of the kids sold some of their bread for cigarettes or sugar beets, the beets consisted of only water, by eating the beets, they did get swollen legs and did die. **In** February, the entire camp was placed under quarantine, we all were infected with a virus it was called (dissension fever) spot fever. Every one of us was very sick with high fever.

I was so sick and weak from the high fever, I could not even sit up. Someone brought me some soup, something told me to eat, and if I did not eat, I would never stay alive. Somehow, I forced myself to eat. In a few days, I was able to walk, after three weeks the quarantine ended; moreover, we never went back to the factory.

The fever took its toll, most of the boys in camp did not survive, and I lost many of my friends. Those who survived the fever were selected to work, digging trenches to prevent tanks and other large equipment to pass over them. The digging was very hard and exhausting.

The SS guards were right on top of us and would not let us breathe for a minute. We became more and more frightened because we did not know what was going to happen to us. Somehow, I never gave up hope. I wanted desperately to see my family, to learn what happened to them. I especially wanted to see my twin brother because I felt so close to him. Somehow, I never gave up hope.

In the middle of March 1945, the snow began to melt.

They selected me with ninety-nine other men to clean up an army camp. We had no idea where we were going, we lined up four in a row, and accompanied by six SS guards, we started out walking at six in the morning. We were walking too fast for the kids in the rear of the column, and they had to run to keep up. The SS guards kept yelling "Nach slagen" "Nach slagen! Keep up! Keep up! I was walking in the rear of the column and could see that many of the kids just could not keep up.

Two of us tried to help one of the boys to keep up, but after five minutes, we could not help any more. The SS guard ordered us to leave him at the side of the road. As we walked away, we heard a gunshot.

The melting snow had turned the road to mud making it very difficult to walk. A couple of us tried to help another boy, but again we had to leave him at the side of the road where he was soon shot by the SS guard. We tried to help another boy, but once again, we were not successful.

Then I realized that I did not have the strength to help anymore so I went to the very front of the column where I continued to hear shots being fired, I felt helpless because I could do nothing about it.

Exhausted, we finally arrived at our destination, to find that we had lost twenty-seven boys along the way. Again we were very sad knowing what happened, and what is going to happen.

We looked at each other, not knowing who would be next. As we arrived there, we found food that was left over, enough to feed everyone. It took us six hours, we cleaned up the camp and began our journey back. Luckily, we lost no one on our return back to camp.

Everyday more and more kids were dying from hunger and exhaustion. Whenever someone died, two boys were selected to take the corpse to the crematorium. I always tried to hide when they made these assignments, but finally I was unable to avoid this terrible job.

It's something I will never forget. There were four bodies; we had to take them to the crematorium. After we were finished, we had to pick up some bread for the camp. That was the best thing that happened to my friend and me. We actually were in the rear of the truck with the bread. My friend and I ate one of the bread and were able to get back a little of our strength.

On May 2, 1945, the few off us who were left were loaded into trucks, not knowing where they were taking us. Strangely enough, we were not scared any more. We felt that now everything was in God's hand. He would determine our fate, whether we would live or die.

However, we still had faith and most of all hope. In a few hours, we arrived at a new camp; the name of the camp was Dornau. We all got off the trucks; they ordered us into the camp.

We discovered many people were lying in their bunks very sick. This place was calld the death camp. We found out that these kids where given only one meal a day. Those who could walk to pick up their food and eat and those who were too sick to move, ate very little.

Next day they picked some of us to do some work on the railroad. It was hard and exhausting work. I was hurt and taken back to camp, but I had little time to rest. A few days later, they ordered me back to work. This time we had to clean up the railroad station.

As we walked back to camp, one elderly SS guard asked us where we came from. One of the boys answered Poland, another from Czechoslovakia, and I am from Hungary. Than he wanted to know what part of Hungary! I told him Transilvania. He ask me if I spoke Romanian and when I said yes we talked some and I found out he was seventy-five years old and he was Romanian.

Next day after work, the Romanian SS guard called me over to talk to me. He asked me how old I was, I told him nineteen year old. Then he told me in German; "Die sonne scheint fur uns heute und morgen Es scheint fur sei." (The sun shines for us today and tomorrow it will shine for you.) Abruptly he turned around and walked away.

I told everyone what the guard told me and that night nobody slept. The lights never went on, and we could not wait for the morning to come.

THANK GOD DARK ENDED.

A New Light Has Begun.

LIGHT

Never shall I forget that night, in camp.

Never shall I forget the Nazis who murdered all those mothers, fathers, brothers, sisters, and children, whose bodies I saw transformed into smoke under a silent sky.

Never shall I forget those flames that consumed my faith forever.

Never shall I forget that smoke.

Never shall I forget those moments that murdered my soul and turned my dreams to ashes,

Never shall I forget those things.

Never shall I forget, as long I live.

Never . . .

Despite the anguish, hardship and brutality inflicted on my mother, father, sisters, brothers, and children, by the Nazis, the only people I hate are individuals I know are my enemies.

People ask me if I hate the Germans. I tell them that I am not a man to generalize. If your father killed my brother, why should I kill his son . . . ? I feel that the biggest sin is to generalize people.

On the morning of May 8, 1945, as soon it got light, we could see that there were no SS guards in camp. I knew we were free. I was the first who dared to go to the gate and open it; four other boys, followed. I felt no happiness, or joy, I was just relieved to be free. My first thought was my twin brother and the rest of my brothers, family and friends.

As we walked down the road, we encountered about twenty German soldiers on horses running past us. We were very scared thinking they were after us. Later we found out that they were running away from the Russian army The Germans where very much afraid of the Russians and they were running to the Americans.

As we walked a woman approached us and offered us food, and told us in German," Ich bin kein Nazi." (I am not a Nazi). We all had a glass of milk and she told us that the war was over. Some of the men who went out after us, they ate too much and they did get very sick and they did die, we told them not to eat too fast and too much.

We did not want to go back to the camp. The five of us decided to go where the SS guard had their headquarters, On the way to the abandoned SS headquarters, we saw German women on the street giving the men from camp food. We told them to give them only milk and a slice of bread or cake. Fortunately we were smart not to eat too much.

We did ask one of the women where we could get some new clothes to wear. She told us that there is a warehouse just down the road. We went there, it was open but nobody was there. The place was very large filled with clothing and food. The first thing we did was get undressed and put on clean underwear and new clothes. We even found a bicycle, we loaded it with things we needed and took off. As we walked, we encountered Russian soldiers; one of them approached us and demanded that we give him the bicycle.

We argued and we tried to explain to him that we were Jewish slave laborers who just been freed. As we argued, it was our luck an officer came over and he ordered the soldier go back in line, and allowed us to go our way. Finally, we arrived at the SS headquarters and found it a very nice place to relax and eat some of the food we had taken from the warehouse.

Later that afternoon a German woman came in to the building crying, she said that she and her daughter were living alone in a house nearby and were very much afraid that the Russian soldiers would harm them. She asked us if we would come, with her and stay in the house as long as we wished. We told her that we would think it over and let her know later. After she left, we talked about what we should do. Three of my friends did not want to go because of what the Germans had done to our fathers, mothers, brothers and sisters, and relatives.

They did not feel we should defend any German. One of the boys was very sick and he did not care either way what we decided to do. I tried to persuade my friends to stay with the two women. I told them there was some good and bad in all of us, and we saw it right in the camp where we came from. I said that the only ones we should hate are the ones we know are bad.

Finally, everyone agreed to go, and I think we all felt good about that. Next day we moved in. The Russians went to houses and they gathered girls to peel potatoes and do all kind of work. All the females where the Russians occupied were very frightened of them.

Now my only thoughts were how to get home and wondering who I would find there, I was especially anxious to know if my twin brother would be there. After resting a week, I went to the Town of Waldenburg to get some Identification paper, so I could travel across the borders. After I got the ID papers, I had to find out how to travel, because I had no idea of how to get home.

After searching around for a while, I found some Italian prisoners who were going home, from their camp were all going to Bratislava, in Czechoslovakia, which was in the general direction, I was going. I told them that I was going to Bratislava. They were happy to take me with them. I did not go to the Russians for help, as long I had transportation, and my papers to travel. I packed a few things I had, and said good-bye to my dear friends and left.

When I got there, there were twenty five trucks ready for the journey. They all welcomed me; we all loaded into the trucks. The journey lasted about four hours. When I got to Bratislava, I did see a city in ruins. I had to walk to the far end of the city to the train station where I boarded the train to take me to Budapest. In Hungary I was so tired that I fell fast asleep on the train. When I woke, all my belongings were gone, I was left with nothing.

As I got off the train, I spotted a large sign that read, "Welcome Home Shalom". I found out that a Jewish agency was in the city, so I went there right away. Shortly after walking into the office, somebody recognized me, and told me that they had seen four of my brothers in Cluj, and they were waiting for me. The agency gave me some money and ticket for the train. I could not wait to get on the train to Cluj.

Somehow, my brothers learned about my arrival, and Leon, Willie, Fulop, and Alex, they were all waiting for me at the station. My first question was, "did you hear anything about my twin brother Martin, and Sulem? They told me that Martin was in Dachou concentration Camp, and was very sick and no one had heard anything about Sulem. I asked about my two cousins and their families but no one had heard anything. They knew what happened to our father, mother, and two sisters, nephews and brother Shlomo.

They took me to the house where they were living which was not very far from the station. Next day I was very anxious to see the house we were forced to leave behind, the house was there; some family lived in it. I was afraid to tell them that I lived here. My two cousins houses were also occupied. I went back and asked my brothers if they did anything about our house, they told me not yet, because they were waiting for Sulem to come home, and he will take care of the house. Sulem was the one who build the house. They thought that was his house.

My brothers did take care of me very well, they did give me everything I needed, but I was very unhappy and sad. Because after two weeks, went by and I did not hear anything from Martin and Sulem. After many thoughts, I knew that my brothers would not take care of me forever, so I decided to leave in search for my twin brother. I packed my belongings and left for the train station, without saying a word to my brothers. While waiting for the train, my brothers showed up and wanted to know where I was going.

I told them that I wanted to look for Martin and Sulem.

They begged me to wait a little longer, maybe Martin, and Sulem would show up very soon. They also told me when my brother Martin will show up, then we could decide what to do. In the meantime, they said that they would do everything possible to take good care of me. I did give in, and went home with them. After a few days living with my brothers, I was very lonesome all my friends were gone and I felt I wanted to do something for myself.

After all, I thought how much longer they would want to support me. I heard nothing about my twin brother Martin and Sulem, who was my favorite brother, because he was the only brother who really did help my parents with the household. I knew that I could not wait around any longer. On July 1945, I found out that there was a ship soon leaving for Israel.

I knew in order to leave my brothers, I had to join a group who were leaving Romania and going to Israel, and I joined them. Also I knew joining that group I could travel and look for my brothers, Sulem, and Martin. Now I had a good chance to leave on a transport with other girls and boys from all over country. They told me to be ready to leave in a few days. I did give them a different address to call me so that my brothers would not know that I was leaving.

In a few days, they contacted me to make sure that I was ready in preparation to leave. I had already taken my clothes to a friend's house. They also registered me to go to Israel. One day before I was to leave, I told my brothers that I was going to stay with my friend, for the night. The next morning at five o'clock, we had to be at the station. At six-thirty the train left for Hungary. In Hungary, we received papers to go to Vienna; (Austria) the city had four zones: American, British, French, and Russian. Now we had to get new papers to leave Vienna. The next day we went to the American Consulate to get the new papers to allow us to travel.

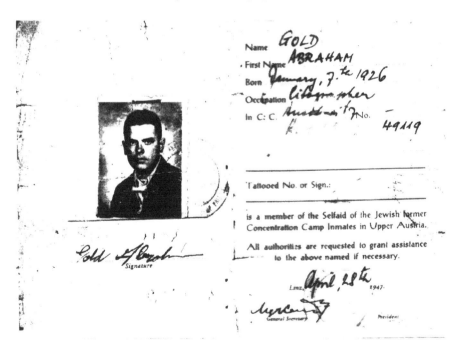

MEMBER'S
IDENTITY CARD

Now that we had all the papers, we boarded the train to go to a little Austrian town called Wels in the American zone. In Wels there was a large displaced persons camp, (DPC). There were many refugees from all over Poland, Czechoslovakia, and Hungary. Some of the refugees were very sick and some of them went home, and some of them did not have any family left, they were waiting to go to America, Israel, or any Country, where able to emigrate. The following day I inquire about my twin brother; there were not any answers, only that he was sick. While searching for my twin brother, with great joy and surprise I could not believe my eyes when, I saw my brother Sulem.

We hugged each other tears were running down our cheeks, he was my favorite brother. The first thing he asked me was where is Martin I was silent. I did not know what to say, because I heard all kinds of stories, that he was very sick. Then I told him everything I knew; how Martin and I were separated, and how I was separated from my parents, sisters, and nephews, he knew already what happened, to our parents, our sisters, and nephews in Auschwitz.

I told him how I went home and, found four of our brothers, Leon, Willy, Fulop, and Alex. In addition, told him why I had left them. Sulem was ready to go home, the next day I told him to take good care of himself, and that he should keep in touch with me. I told him that he should sell the house it belongs to you. I stayed in the D.P.C. In the camp they did provide us with food and some clothes. I did not like doing nothing. I did not know how much longer, we had to wait. To go to Israel, was very uncertain, because of the British or to go to the U.S.A.

I just could not wait around so in August 1945, I went into town to the American army headquarters looking for a job. Luck was with me and I got a job in the kitchen. I did not care as long I had a job and not have to rely on camps food. A few months later the army told me to move in to the American headquarter I was very happy working for the Americans, and lived there too. I did not care as long I was able to get away from the D P camp and did not have to rely on their food and clothing.

Before I moved in I had to take a medical examination, they also gave me American clothes

This picture was taken at the D P camp with my new uniform
it made me very proud and happy

From August 1945, to March 1946, we did not require any working papers. In March 1946, all the displace persons who lived in the city, had to register and get working papers

This is the work document for the non-citizens

In April 1946, I got a job in the army motor pool as a mechanic. There I learned to drive a jeep, and October of that year, an army captain a good friend of mine offered me a job in the Army P.X. Post exchange. Meanwhile I was corresponding with my brothers, trying to find out if they had heard anything from my twin brother. They had no news but send me the address of an uncle who lived in the United States—in New York.

I wrote to my uncle telling him that I was his nephew, and for a while, we corresponded. I informed the (Hebrew Immigrant Aid Society HIAS) that I had an uncle in the United States. I needed a sponsor if I was to emigrate. I asked my uncle if he would sponsor me, and to send me the papers, I needed to come to the United States. But after that letter, I never heard from him again I wrote to him several times, but he never answered my letters. The last letter I sent my uncle and asked him the reason for not writing. People continued to leave the camp, some to the United States some to Canada, and some to other countries.

In May 1947, the D.P. camp closed. The few who were left in camp, went to another camp in a town called Linz, and the other half to Bad

Gasthein I remained in Wels working for the American P.X. I continued to write to my brothers to find out if they heard anything more about Martin, and told them what I experienced with our uncle in America. They told me not to give up hope. Here I was all alone, all my friends gone. I wrote to the HIAS and explained what happened with my uncle. They told me they were going to get in touch with him themselves, so I waited and waited, I had no choice.

In Wels, there were four Jewish boys and about fourteen American Jewish soldiers. We all went to Linz to the DP camp for the High Holidays. I met a couple of my old friends there, and they told me that many of the boys I knew had left for Italy, and from there they went to Israel.

After the Holidays, we all returned to Wels. I did not know what to do. Should I wait to hear from my uncle in America or sign up to go to Israel? In October 1947, the P.X. and the American Army left Wels.

Now I had to do something,—go to Linz, or Bad-Gasthein. I called the HIAS and told them that my intentions were to go to Bad—Gastein they informed me that I could stay there, but to be in touch with them. When I arrived in Bad-Gastein, I found very few of my friends there. They told me that one transport had just left for Israel, and they did not know when another transport would leave. I stayed in a very nice hotel. Meanwhile I kept in touch with the HIAS.

I never lost hope or faith. In September 1948, I went back to Wels, now I really had to look for a job. If I wanted to stay in Wels, and I did get a job in a Zuckerfabrik. Then in November, the HIAS called and told me and fifteen other boys to make sure we had proper identification with us, and to be ready to go to Salzburg for a medical exam.

They informed us that we were being prepared to go to the United States all of us were excited and happy. We just could not believe it was true. The first thing I did was to write to my brothers to tell them the good news. I told them that as soon as I will hear the exact time I would be leaving, I would write again.

It did not take long. I got a letter from the HIAS telling me to be ready to go to Salzburg on November 25 for a typhus test, and again on December 1st for more testing.

After a few days, the HIAS notified me, to be ready to go to Salzburg, and to bring all the documents with me, and tickets for a ship leaving Bremen Haven for the United States. Now that I received the papers, I was very excited, first thing I did was to write to my brothers the good news.

They responded immediately with a very long letter.

They told me now, that my twin brother Martin passed away one week after the liberation, but they did not want to tell me at that time because of everything I had gone through. Now that I was leaving Europe for the States, they thought, it was only right for me to know the truth about my twin brother, I was devastated. I read the letter repeatedly and cried and cried. On December 27, we left for Bremen Haven. There was a large camp. When we arrived they gave me my Visa to the United States and I found out that the HIAS had sponsored me, not my uncle.

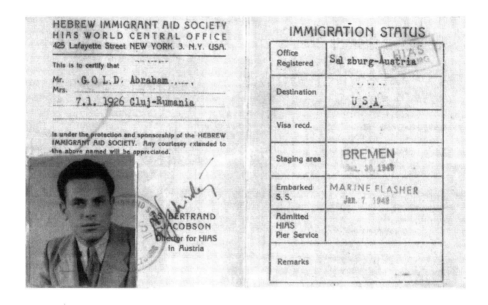

This was my Visa to the U.S.A.

On January 7 my nineteenth birthday, I began a new life, as I set my foot on the ship SS Marine Flasher bound for the United States of America. The fun started as we got on the ship. We tried to guess who would get sick first. About three hours after supper, one of the passengers got sick and that started it off. Almost half the ship did not show up for breakfast. At my table, only my friend and I showed up.

This picture, was taken during the safety exercises

After the exercises, everybody came down to eat; I met a nice girl on the ship, from Lithuania, We had a good time, but some of my friends did not approve of her because she was not Jewish. I told them to mind their own business and not to worry and that I was just having fun. On the seventh day at sea, we were hit by a big storm and everyone, got sick again. At this time, people got hurt, with broken hands and legs; it was very frightening. One day we found out that we were going to Boston, we were all very disappointed because we thought that the ship was going to New York.

Then I learned that everyone would leave the ship in Boston, but not everyone would remain there. The group that I belonged to, the HIAS was going to New York. That news made me very happy because all my friends were going there too.

The long journey ended on January 17. We were all very excited. As we got off the ship, many people were waiting on the dock. There were a lot of kisses and hugs. I was very touched and happy for those people. Those of us, who were going to New York, were taken to the railroad station. On the train, I thought about who might be waiting for me. It really did not matter because, I was just so happy to be in the United States that nothing else mattered.

The train arrived in Grand Central Station, and there were many people waiting at the station. It was very exciting. Everyone I knew seemed to have somebody waiting for him or her. Someone from the HIAS came over to me and asked me if my name was Gold or Preisler. I told him that my name was Abraham Gold.

Then he said that my uncle, and aunt, and two cousins were waiting for me. Was I surprised! When I saw them, we hugged and kissed each other.

They told me they rented a room for me in the building where they lived, and that I was going to eat with them. The following day my aunt took me to see the show at Radio City Music Hall. First thing was to register to go to school to learn English, next thing I did was to register for citizenship.

A week later my uncle took me to learn the furrier trade; I did not like it, because I wanted to get a job in my trade as an offset printer. However, at the same time, I had to get a job February 1945 I did get a job in Alexander's Department, in the hosiery stock room. My salary was $27.00 a week. The first week I kept my salary. After that, I paid $10.00 a week for my rent. Soon my uncle told me that my aunt wasn't feeling well and I had better find somewhere else to eat, but he invited me to eat with his family every Friday.

It was then that I asked my uncle why he did not write to me while I was in Europe. I did write to you and did ask you if I did anything wrong, but no answer. Now I knew that I addressed my letters "Dear Uncle and family" and not "dear Aunt and Uncle," so I thought maybe I had insulted my aunt and I told my uncle I was sorry if this was a mistake on my part. However, I told him I thought it was very cruel not to answer my letters, and that I and my brothers were the only ones left alive, and he had been my only hope of being able to come to America. In addition, I told him that if it were not for the HIAS, I would not be here. Every time my uncle saw me, he always asked about my family. I never knew my grandfather or grandmother, and never did talk about them. I had very few answers for his many questions because I was the youngest in the family, and I was 14 years old when I left my parents and went to an apprentice school and at 18 years old I was deported to Auschwitz. I was not aware in the questions he would ask me, as I was too young at the time.

A few months later, I decided that I could not take any more of my uncle's endless questions. He questioned me, as if I were not his nephew. Therefore, I began to look for my own apartment. 'With G-d's help, I located a nice Hungarian family who rented me a room for fifteen dollars a week, including breakfast. In August, I moved into my new apartment. One Friday night I had a date with a nice girl, and I forgot to tell my aunt I was not coming to dinner. After that, my invitation for Friday's dinner was ended. I might also add the entire time I was in my uncle's house he never bought me anything. However, they once gave me an old suit that belonged to my cousin.

I still called them once a week. The store (Alexander's) I worked in promised me an increase in salary after six months. After the six months, I asked them for a raise in my salary I did not get it. Instead, they gave me two weeks to look for another job. I decided to look for a job in my own trade.

A friend of mine who lived in the same building told me about someone who had an offset printing shop. I took off from work one day and went over there. It was a one man's shop. The name was Ben's offset printing. He was working all alone. He told me he could use some help. I got the job and he paid me $35.00 a week. In August, 1945, I quit Alexander's and went to work for Ben's offset printing. I was very happy to be working in my own trade.

I wrote to my brothers about my job, and asked if possible, I would like them to send me my certificate that said I belonged to the International Printing Union. In a couple of months, I received the certificate in the mail. In November, I went to the Union offices and told them that I belonged to the I.P.U. in Romania. They asked me if I was working and where, and I told them. Then they called my boss and asked him why he did not tell them that I was working for him. The next day when I went to work, my boss told me what happened. He told me that he had a union shop and they were very strict about who could work there.

Although he was very sorry, he would have to let me go. So now in December, I had to look for another job. It was very hard to get a job in my trade if you did not know somebody and I knew no one. I decided that my best bet was to go to HIAS. Maybe they could help me. The people at HIAS interviewed me and told me to come back in a week. I had no choice but to wait. Meanwhile, I had to pay my rent and eat. A week went by and I went to HIAS again. They said that they were looking for a job for me. I told them that I had no money, and was no longer staying with my uncle and since the HIAS had brought me to the United States I was relying on them to help me. Again, they told me to be patient and as soon as they find me a job, they would call. Fortunately, the family where I stayed saw what I was going through, and they told me that I could stay in my place until I got a job.

Once I was working, I could pay them what I owed them. I felt very fortunate to have met such nice people. After another week passed, I could wait no longer. Therefore, I went to another Jewish organization called JOINT. They gave me the same story. I just could not believe it. I did not know where to run. I was in a desperate situation. Luckily, for me, the family I lived with true friends and they gave me encouragement to go on. A few days later, in February I got a call from HIAS about a job.

The job was a tool and die maker which was not my trade, but I had no choice. I needed to work to pay back all the money I owed, but I would continue to look for a job in my trade. One day, while working at a punch press, an accident occurred and some of my fingers were crushed. I immediately grabbed my hand and squeezed with my right hand to stop the bleeding.

My boss took me out of the building and found a cab to take me to the hospital emergency room. When the doctor came in, he asked me what happened and told me to show him my hand. As I released my right hand to show him, my left hand I fainted. The only thing I remember was that I awoke the next morning to find my hand in a cast. I had no idea how much damage there was to my hand in the cast. I just hoped that everything would be all right. The only person who came to see me was the son of the family where I lived.

When he came, they asked him who he was looking for. He told them, "My brother." However, when they asked him my name, for a moment he lost his memory he was so confused that he could not remember my name and they would not allow him to see me.

He came back the next day and was able to see me. I told him to call my uncle and tell him what happened to me. When he got home, he told his parents all about what happened to me, and they told my uncle. The fourth day I was in the hospital, my uncle showed up. I told him what happened, but he never asked me how I was getting along or if I needed anything. After seven days, they released me from the hospital. My hand was still in the cast.

The doctor told me that they did the best they could, and in about six weeks, they would remove the cast. However, I had to come back every second week for an examination. After the second examination, they told me that everything looked good. My only fear was that I did not know how the damage to my hand would affect my future and my work. I wrote to my brothers about what happened to me and told them about how my uncle and I were not getting along too well. I told them how he questioned me about my family, and I thought he was always doubtful I was his nephew. I think that was the main reason he was so cold to me and did not care what happened to me.

Thank God I was a survivor, and I knew that I would survive again no matter what. The time came to take the cast off my hand. I was scared because I did not know what I was going to see. It was not as bad as I thought, but I did lose part of my three fingers. Because I knew what the hand looked like, I was no longer as scared as I had been before. Now I still had to support myself, but I could not do much with one hand. In April,

I did get Workman Compensation money it was $ 34.00 a week. A cousin of mine had a butcher shop, so I went to him and he hired me as a delivery boy. It was great. I had something to do with my time.

I was able to enjoy myself a little, and I would go to the 92nd Street YMHA where I met some boys and girls and I became friendly with them. After a few months, my hand began to get better. I started to look for a job in the printing field, and found one in a mailing house working on a small printing press I could handle. Six months after my accident, I got my draft notice from the Army, and had to report for a physical examination.

I went to the Compensation Board, and told them that the army drafted me, and I would like to settle my accident. They did settle and they gave me $3.000.00. Two weeks later, on September 28, 1950, I had to report to the 34th street armory. They selected according to their schooling and profession and sent me to the Engineer Training Center at Fort Belvoir, Virginia and I received a $ 10,000.00 life insurance, was required by the United States military.

I am standing in the center of photo

During basic training, I complained about my hand hurting me. My fingers kept getting blue from the cold, and it hurt me a lot. Early in

November, my commanding officer called me to his office and asked me when and how my fingers were injured. Not long after that, I received a notice that on November 18 I would receive an Honorable Discharge. I got my discharge; it was very hard to say goodbye, to the good friends I had made during my basic training. I left the base and returned to New York. I was glad to be home, I missed the very good friends, I made in basic training, but I was glad to be home. After resting for a week, I went back to my old job. While working I kept looking for a better paying job, and in February 1951, I found one. This job gave me the opportunity to work on a large press and make a better salary.

One beautiful Sunday afternoon in April of that year, I decided to go to the 92nd Street Y to see if I could meet some of my friends. When I got to the Y, I was lucky enough to meet some friends that I had not seen for the longest time. We were very happy to see each other, we talked for a while. One of my friends told us about a Purim dance being held in a Hotel. Therefore, we all decided to go there and maybe we meet some girls. We got there it was a very large place, many girls and boys. I danced with some of the girls, and we all had a good time.

Just as we were getting ready to go home, my friends and I spotted, three good-looking girls. We decided to stay for one more dance. Without hesitating, I walked over to who I thought was the nicest looking girl with gorgeous blue eyes and asked her to dance. While we danced, I found out her name was Sylvia. Because I looked Latino, the first thing she asked me was where I came from and where was I born. I quickly told her, "In the United States." She told me that was not true. So then, I told her that my family moved back to Europe when I was very young. She did not believe a word I said.

As the dance ended, I decided very quickly that I had better tell her the truth. Therefore, I asked her if she would like to have a drink. She agreed, and then excused herself for a moment. Meanwhile, I ordered the drinks. I waited and waited for her to return, and after ten minutes or more, I almost gave up.

Just as I got up to look for her, she appeared. Was I happy to see her again! We did not stop talking and I told the whole truth about me from the beginning to the end. We were the last ones left in the dance hall. Therefore, I went to the coatroom to get our coats. I helped her with her coat and she took mine and helped me put it on. We heard the woman from the coatroom say, "That is true love." As we were walking out, I asked her if I could take her home and she said, "Yes." I flagged down a cab and took her home.

Before leaving her, I asked for her telephone number.

I waited a whole week before I called her. I asked her if she would like to go to the theater. She responded favorably, which made me very happy. The following week we went to the theater. We had a wonderful time that I will never forget. The following week I met her parents who seemed to be very nice. After that, we called each other very often. We saw each other every day for lunch, because my job was right across the street, from where dear Sylvie was employed.

We saw each other every Saturday and Sunday. It was love from the very beginning. After six weeks, I asked Sylvie if she would marry me. Without hesitating, she said, "Yes!" Then we hugged and kissed each other. After that, we went home and asked her parents blessing. They were very happy. The following week, I introduced my dear Sylvie to my aunt, uncle, and their children. We told them of our plans, and they wished us good luck. We could not decide when to get married.

We had our vacation coming soon, so we decided to get married, on July 1 1951. We had six weeks to get ready and we made it. During this time, we looked for a place to live, and found a two-room apartment in the Bronx. Now we did look at a Catering hall and luckily we did find one near her parents.

We had about forty couples, including my aunt, uncle and their children, and three couples were my friends. The rest of the guests were family and friends of my lovely Sylvie.

During the ceremony, we had a special memorial service for my mother, father, sisters, and brothers. Everybody was in tears; I really missed them very much. Following the wedding, we went on a two-week honeymoon to the Catskill Mountains. When we returned from our honeymoon, we stayed in a motel while looking for furniture for our new apartment. A week later, we moved in to our newly furnished apartment. In March 1952, we found out that my dear Sylvie was pregnant and we were very happy.

One month before giving birth, my dear Sylvie stopped working. Then on October 14, 1952, our daughter was born and we named her Blima (Barbara) after my dear mother. Soon I began looking for a better paying job. I got lucky and found a very good job at a very good salary. After six months, I got a raise because the boss appreciated the good work that I was doing. Then in February 1954 our second daughter was born, we named her leeba (Lesley) after my dear wife's aunt.

Now I had to look for a larger apartment. One day a sales clerk, where I worked asked me if I would like to go into business for myself. He explained to me that he knew a company looking for a partner who was a good press operator, and had experience on a Royal Zenith press. This sounded good to me because I had experience with that press. However, there was only one problem. They wanted $4,000.00 for someone to come into the business, which I did not have.

My wife I talked it over and we decided to approach her parents for a loan. We did not have any luck. We ultimately approached my dear wife's aunt for a loan. We promised to pay her two hundred dollars every month until the loan was paid, and she did agree.

In May 1955, I became a partner in an offset printing business. In September of that year, I received a letter from my brother Willy, who asked me to be his sponsor so that he and his family could emigrate to the United States. He said the HIAS would take care of paperwork. Since I had my own business, I was able to send the sponsorship papers for Willie and family to come to the States. My brother Sulem and his family had gone to Israel.

My other three brothers were still in Romania. In a few months later, my brother Willie, and his family arrived in the United States This time HIAS did its job and took care of my brother's family. In summer 1956, I rented a bungalow in the Catskill Mountains. We had only a kitchen and bedroom, and I felt very sad that there was not a bungalow available for my brother and his family. We did find out that bungalow would be available, but for two weeks only, and we took it.

We invited my brother and his family to stay there. However, my sister-in-law was not satisfied. She complained to some people in the bungalow colony that we should be helping them out because I had been here many years and owned my own business.

However, it turned out that my brother had much more than anyone thought he had. He had brought out of Europe, china, silver, and many other valuable items. They were not poor, but by complaining, they made everybody believe they had nothing. The partnership in the offset printing business did not last long. After two years, I dissolved my partnership. I was working too hard and putting in long hours, but my salary never increased.

In August 1957, I left the business, and for one year, could not go into my own business. In the meantime, I looked for another job. I finally got work and was very happy because I was able to be home with my family, and I was making a good salary. That same year we decided to have another baby. Maybe we would have a boy! In October, my wife became pregnant. A good friend of mine had a photo offset plate-making shop. To expand his business he subleased space in the next building and placed a new Royal Zenith press in that room. He asked me to work part-time when he needed me.

One day a man who did work for him was cleaning the press and a washcloth did catch, in the gear and damaged the press. In addition, some of the gears were broken and the press was only two years old. My friend asked me if I would like to take over that part of his business, and make the payments on the press. He owned $ 13,000.00 on the press, plus $4,000.00 on repairs. First, I called the man who sold my friend the press because I knew him very well.

I told him that I would take over the payments on the press plus the cost to fix it and agreed to pay him $460.00 each mouth for four years. My friend was very grateful to me for taking over the payments; the only thing I had to pay was $1000.00 cash for transferring all the papers to my name. The deal was closed, on May 8, 1958, I opened my own printing shop, and I named it (Superior Offset Corp.) It was a big undertaking for me. Although my friend helped me, I had to work very hard because I ran the press and the same time I had to be a sales clerk.

On May 29, 1958, our son Jeffrey was born. We named him after his grandfather Jacob. It was one of the many happy days of our lives, having two lovely girls and a boy. Now we had to look for a three-bedroom apartment, for our expanding family. We found one in the same building where we were living. One day our daughter Barbara came home from school all wet and crying because a kid had thrown her in the gutter. We decided to look for a better neighborhood, and in the meantime, we enrolled the two girls in Beth Miriam, a Jewish school for girls.

We were visiting a relative of mine and he told us that he just purchased a house in Orangeburg, New York, which is in Rockland County, not far from the city. He said that he only had to put down 10%, which was $2,500.00 the following week, we went to see the house, our relative bought, and it was beautiful. While there we did see a house for sale, it was a two-year-old colonial, and we did inquire about the house.

The mortgage and insurance came to $160.00 a month. This was less than the cost of a large apartment in the Bronx. Now my thoughts were how I would commute to work, I would need transportation to work in the city. Two cousins of mine told me not to worry, because they were going to have a carpool. Therefore, we decided to buy the house, and on June 19 1962, we moved into our new home. It was a big step for us. Our car pool started, but lasted a few weeks.

The reason I could not meet the designated time because I had to work late. Since we had only one car, I had to take the bus to work, and it was a hardship. As business did get better, I was able to buy another car. Soon after moving to Orangeburg, we did join the Orange town Jewish Center, and the Andrew Goldstein Post 731, J.W.V. In the same year, I made the last payment, I was able to save some money; I moved to a larger quarter and bought another press.

It took me another four years to pay off the press. At the same time, Hungary was having a revolution. My brother Alex was able to take his wife and his two children to the border to Austria. Alex went back to Budapest to retrieve some of his belongings. As he got in the house, the Russians arrested him. After two months, my sister-in-law immigrated to the U.S.A., Two years later, with much effort from the U.S.A., my brother Alex was free and was able to immigrate to the U.S.A., and joined his wife and his two children.

After a few months later, I sent papers to my brother Leon and his family, to immigrate to the U.S.A. It took a few months and they came to the U.S.A. On March 27, 1966, my dear wife gave birth to a sweet little girl who we named Karen, after our uncle Kalman. Now we had to build a family room and enlarge the dining room in our house. In 1967, we had an oil boycott and the gasoline lines were very long. We had to wait a half-hour to fill the car tank. A friend of mine who had a shop and he lived in Spring Valley told me that he is taking the train to work. Although I lived in Orangeburg five years, I did not know that there was a train from Spring Valley to Hoboken NJ. To save gas but I did not save time I drove to the station, and the whole trip to work took almost two hours.

Here, my dear Sylvie inserts the Commanders Pin.

Here, my dear Sylvie inserts the Commanders Pin.

1969 I served as POST Commander and since I joined the J. W. V. I held a seat on the J.W.V. County Council. I also served as Judge Advocate and as a member of the Executive Committee.

I was also active in the causes for Israel, and the Soviet Jewry. In July 1970, Sylvie and I took a trip to Israel to visit with my brother Sulem. I had not seen him in twenty five years. What a great feeling, it was to see him again; he had always been my favorite brother! In June 1971, we celebrated our son's Bar Mitzvah, and in 1972, our daughter Barbara got married.

Soon after, my last brother Fulop arrived, which made me very happy. He was my last brother, to arrive in the United States He was not married. In 1973, for a Bar Mitzvah gift, we took our son on a tour of Europe to see the house that we built in Cluj.

We arrived in Bucharest (Romania) we rented a car and drove to Transilvania. On our way to Cluj, we were searching for the Dracula's castle. We came across an old church where a ruler of Romania lived and he was very wicked. When we arrived in Cluj, we found a cousin of mine who told us the sad news of how he lost his whole family. The house we built was still there. Sylvie and my son could not believe I lived in such a small house without water or electricity. I asked about all the Jewish neighbors, and was met with silence. We all cried, after a while he told us that in the city, very few Jews where left and the few youngsters went to Israel. There were only a few older folks left, about 70 people where there was once twenty thousand here. A kosher kitchen provided, food for the few who ate only kosher food, sponsors of the United Jewish Appeal. I also ask what happened to all the synagogues as only one was left where there had been six

From Cluj we wanted to go to Hungary. We needed a special visa and we had to go to Belgrade, (Yugoslavia) to the American Council. We got a visa for only three days. Unfortunately, we ran out of money. The councilor told us to send a telegram to a friend in the United States to send us money to the Hungarian, Nation bank in Budapest. As we got off the train, in Budapest, I saw a cab driver and I went over to him and told him I had no money to stay at a hotel for the night. The driver said he just separated from his wife. He invited us to stay in his house until we got the money. Fortunately I spoke Hungarian.

The following day we went to the bank. The money finally came in the third day. Now that we had the money, we checked into a hotel for one night. In the restaurant I asked the waiter if there were any Jews left, he said thank God not too many with them, I told him I am Jewish, and left without giving a tip. We visited the Dohany utca Synagogue. The fourth day we left for Romc before the border the train stopped. Two Hungarian and one Russian border guard, checked our visas. They asked why we stayed over one day.

They took me off the train. My wife and son were scared. I explained to them, the reason we stayed another day, The guard asked me if I had any Hungary money with me I told them I had some, they told me at the border I could spend my money. They let me go. Sylvie and Jeffrey were delighted to see me. We could not wait, to go to Rome and fly to the United States.

After being in business for twenty years, I started to lose some of my best customers. I found out that one of these customers left me because they really wanted to buy my business. I had no choice but to negotiate with them. In 1979, I sold my business to Crown Sample Card, with one condition. They had to give me a five-year contract as a supervisor in the company,

After I sold my business, I took a three-week vacation to Israel. This time my dear brother Sulem was not there as he passed away a year before. As my fifth year as supervisor was ending I requested another five year contract, but the company refused. I had only one option join the printers union. My boss did not like that; I joined the union and he told me that I would lose my two weeks of vacation time and my pension. I did not care, and I joined the union.

When summer came, I requested my vacation and they refused me. I went to the union to complain, they claimed that I only joined the union nine months ago. Therefore, they could not do anything for me. My next action was to go to the National Labor Relation Board to complain. In April 1983, they sent my company an order to allow me to have my vacation, with one condition; I had to take one week at a time. The same year, our daughter Lesley got married. Then in 1987, I retired, a year before my 62nd birthday. In 1988, we sold our house, and bought a townhouse in the Pocono Mountains in Pennsylvania. The following year, our daughter Karen got married in England.

After resting for a few months, I had to do something good. I found out that not far from our house, was an emergency service, called West End Ambulance, and they needed volunteers,. Now I had a good chance to do something good and save lives. I felt, that because my own life had been spared from the horrors of Europe, and the United States of America had been so good to me, and my family. I wanted to give something back. I went to the ambulance station to inquire if I could be a volunteer. The only thing they required was a doctor's certificate of my health. I brought a certificate, and I was accepted.

I had to go through ninety day training program and if I passed the training, they would accept me. The training was a big challenge. I was determined to go through the training. I had to learn first aid and CPR. I passed and was accepted. I received my uniform. I was very excited and happy.

In 1990 our son Jeffery get married

The First row from Left I am the fourth

The job was not too exciting as an EMS so I decided to take examination for EMT. Now I really did experience the job. I saved many lives, and made many people very happy. In addition, I responded to an automobile accident where the victim was a skinhead, I attended to his wounds.

Afterward I told him that I am a Jew, and he looked at me and did give me a hug and did thank me. A week later he visited me at the station. We became good friends.

It was a tough and demanding job, however it was very satisfying, knowing I was helping the wounded and sick, and I was saving many lives.

This picture was taken, at a West End October fest.

I did take a driver's test, did pass, and certified to drive an ambulance. Now I served for another four years.

Here I am in front of the building with my new Ambulance.

September 1997, it was time for me to quit the Ambulance, service. For appreciation of my service I received a bronze plaque with a beautiful inscription that recognized my service

This is the plaque I received on my retirement.

1998, we moved to West Palm Beach, Florida. I had to start writing my story in earnest. Here again I volunteered with the VA Hospital. One day as a shuttle driver and another day I helped with filling the soda and candy machines. After doing a good job with volunteering, I was asked if

I would take a full time job with payment. The person I helped did quit. With consideration. I accepted but only 15 hours a week. I had to go thru a health examination, which I passed. They hired me and I worked five hours a day, three days a week with no help as I was promised. The job did not last too long as it needed a full time worker. After six months I told them to get someone who would work full time and gave my two week notice. It took them a long time to replace me. Soon after I volunteered in the canteen which was the stock room where I priced the merchandise.

Special Contribution Award

Presented to

Abe Gold

for

Excellence

in fulfilling the mission of
The Veterans Canteen Service.

Outstanding Canteen of the Year Award
2004
West Palm Beach, FL

Director, Veterans Canteen Service

DEPARTMENT OF VETERANS AFFAIRS
Veterans Canteen Service
Central Office
St. Louis, MO 63125-4194

In Reply Refer To

March 31, 2005

Mr. Abe Gold
Veterans Canteen Service #548
VA Medical Center
West Palm Beach, FL

Dear Mr. Gold,

Congratulations on being a part of the winning team in our Annual Canteen of the Year Award for the period February 1, 2004 to January 31, 2005. This award signifies outstanding individual and team effort in rendering service to our veterans and caregivers "beyond customer expectations."

Your contribution toward enhancing the quality of our service reflects your sincere dedication and devotion to the Veterans Canteen Service and demonstrates your enthusiastic commitment to customer service excellence.

I extend my personal thanks for your efforts toward winning this award.

Sincerely,

James B. Donahoe
Director
Veterans Canteen Service

In 2001, we celebrated our 50th Anniversary, with our children and grandchildren, in a hotel in the Catskill Mountains.

picture is our 50th Anniversary with our Grandchildren.

First row Lesley, Jessica, Sara, Leslie, Ethan, Mathew, Eric, Second row, Karen, Sam, Jeremy, Barbara: Third row: Jimmy, Michael, & friend, David, Barry: Fourth row: Jeff, Danny, & friend, Jarred.

In 2005, we moved to Sebring Florida. to be; closer to our daughter and grandchildren, in Orlando Florida. First thing I did was join the Temple Israel. There I met a lovely lady her name is Dr Lisa Earle, from Austria. We became the best of friends, and she told me that she is from Austria. She also told me how as child she was sent to England. For years, she did not know what ever happened to her parents, lately she did find out that she lost her parents. Recently, she found out her parents and relatives were all lost in the Holocaust. I donated 50 books to the temple which consisted of 44 pages, my autobiographical sketch. Not far from the Temple, there is a Christian School. Soon after I joined the Temple, a teacher found out that I was a Holocaust survivor, the school called the president of the Temple to see if he would contact me and asked if I would speak to the Heartland Christian schoolchildren about my life in the concentration camp. Without any hesitation I responded that I would be honored to speak. In November, 28 in the temple, I spoke to the 11th graders. At that time the temple; sold the books for $10 each. Some of the Children did purchased 18 books: some of the children could not afford the books, however I felt terrible; I went home and looked how many books I still had 18 books left from the 100 books: I took 14 books; I went to the school and did give them the books and told them to give the books to the children that could afford to purchase any books. Given the books to the children, made me feel good.

Students meet Living history

Dark and painful story of holocaust
Experience shared with Dr Lisa Earle

Photos by KATARA SIMMONS/News-Sun

Abraham Gold (above from left), Lisa Earl and Rabbi David Levin speak to Heartland Christian School students about the Holocaust on Tuesday afternoon at Temple Israel in Sebring. Heartland Christian School 11th-graders (at right, from left) Adrienne Gonnella and Chelsea Clark listen closely to Gold's story.

Tale Of Death & Life

A Holocaust Survivor Shares His Experiences With Sebring Students

By MARC VALERO
mvalero@highlandstoday.com

SEBRING — When you want something, you pray.

So he and other incarcerated Jews standing in line before the German officers desperately prayed for their lives. Those picked from the line were never seen again, murdered if they could no longer work, remembered Holocaust survivor Abraham Gold.

"I was praying, don't pick me," Gold continued. "I was lucky."

Sixty-one years later, Gold told his story of survival for the first time in public Tuesday to Heartland Christian School students at Temple Israel. He recently moved to Sebring from West Palm Beach.

While Gold survived the genocide, the massacre took the lives of

Please see TALE on Page 11A ▶

Highlands Today photos by KATHY WATERS

ABOVE: Holocaust survivor Abraham Gold reminisces about his experiences as a Jewish teenager trying to survive life in Nazi prison camps. TOP: Gold has several photos in his personal collection to illustrate his autobiography.

After speaking to the Christian School students in the Temple Israel in Sebring FL November 29th 2005 the following year 2006 Yom Ha'shoah I was invited to speak at the temple Beth David in Spring Hill FL.

A survival tale of hope and anguish

BY MICHELLE JONES
Times Correspondent

SPRING HILL — Abraham Gold's memories are a part of history he hopes the world will never forget.

Gold is a Holocaust survivor.

Yom HaShoah, Holocaust Remembrance Day, was April 14, and congregations around the world observed the day, which was set to mark the anniversary of the Warsaw Ghetto uprising in April 1943. Members of Temple Beth David in Spring Hill welcomed Gold as their guest speaker.

Gold was born in 1926 in Romania. His family of 10 children was raised by loving parents.

At Auschwitz, where he was taken when he was 16, he not only lost his parents, but two brothers, including his twin, and his two sisters.

"I was the only one, in my family, who survived going to the concentration camps," Gold said.

Auschwitz was the largest of its kind, established by the Nazi regime. It was used to incarcerate, to have laborers available for forced labor and to eliminate the Jews in gas chambers and crematoriums.

Gold believes the only reason he survived was because of his faith in God and how he lived one day at a time, hoping for the best.

"I was forced to work in an ammunition factory, separated from my twin, Martin," he said. "That is the reason I don't have a number on my arm."

And, although he remembers the time with sorrow and anguish, he says now the only thing he hates are people who generalize.

"I'm not a man who generalizes," he said. "If someone killed my brother, why should I kill his son? There are good and bad people in all races.

"I remember marching to the train to Auschwitz," said Gold. "There were three different groups watching. One group was clapping, one group was silent and one group was crying."

He also told the story of when he was released from the camp by the Russian Army.

"There was a [German] woman and her daughter who asked for protection," said Gold. "They thought the Russians might harm them. So I stayed with them for a while."

He lived at home with his brothers for a few weeks and then went to Austria until he learned about an uncle who lived in the Bronx.

In 1949 he came to the United States, met and married Sylvia and brought three girls and one boy into the world. Now, his family has 10 grandchildren.

When he lived in New York he started his own offset printing company.

"I've always taken care of myself," he said. "Those were the days when you came up from nothing."

Gold also volunteered with an ambulance corps in Pennsylvania and later at a veteran's hospital in West Palm Beach.

"You feel good when you volunteer," he said.

Sheila Friedman, of Hudson, a member of Temple Beth David, was one of the people who went to hear Gold speak.

She said a good crowd came to the service, including a group from Grace Presbyterian Church.

"That was very nice; it made us feel good (having them come)," she said. "The service was very beautiful and emotional."

But Friedman wondered what people have learned from the Holocaust.

"What is wrong with the human race when we ignore what is going on in Eastern Europe and Africa?" she asked. "Didn't mankind learn anything? It's such a shame."

Holocaust survivor Abraham Gold talks about his experiences at the hands of the Nazis during Yom HaShoah observances at the Temple Beth David in Spring Hill Sunday.

A teacher did hear me speak at the Temple ask me if I would come and speak at the pine View middle school in Zephyrhills. I was delighted to speak to the students in May 2007 I was invited to speak, at the Pine view middle School.

The students wear very delighted and thankful to hear me speak, for appreciation they send me letters.

Here are the few of the letters they send me

Dear Mr Gold,

Thank you so much for comeing and speaking to us. I know it must be hard to talk about it, but I am glad I got to hear your story. I believe more people understand now about that terrifing time. It was much better to hear your story, than stories from books. Thank you once again for telling us your story, and I believe you should keeping telling it to kids for as long as you can!

Thanks a lot,
Jamie Wimies

May 16, 2006

Dear Mr. Gold,

We cannot find the words to thank you enough for taking your time and energy to allow us to share in your life experiences. We wish you a long and happy life.

Dear Mrs. Gold,

Thank you for coming and sharing with us today, it was a pleasure to meet you.

The students at Pine View

Dear Mr. Gold,

I appreciate everything that you've taught us. I understand how hard it must've been for you, and I thank you for talking to us anyways. I will never forget what I've learned from you. Though I will never understand the atrocities of the Holocaust, I can at least try from your words. We are so fortunate to hear your experiences first-hand. Again, thank you.

Sincerely
Wendy G.

Dear Mr. Gold,

I was so inspired to meet you and hear you talk. It is so much better to hear a real life person talk instead of the radio. Thank you for coming, you've inspired so many others, I want to hear and see you give your speech again

Sincerely in your honor,
Mallory M. Reed.

In May 2008 I was invited to speak at the Sebring elementary and high school.

In May 2009 I did speak in Avon park middle and high Schools
In April 14 2010 I was invited to speak at the SFCC
{South Florida Community College}

South Florida workshop participants examine historical photographs as Abraham Gold Holocaust survivor from Hungary, describes his experience during World War II.

In the same year in April 21 2010 I spoke to the students at the Career Academy at the SFCC,

Holocaust survivor visits SFCC

• TUESDAY, MAY 4, 2010 • HIGHLANDS TODAY • f

Abraham Gold, Holocaust survivor, brought Elie Wiesel's memoir "Night" to life on Wednesday, April 21 as he spoke to students at the Career Academy at South Florida Community College.

Photo courtesy of TAYLOR CARSON

AVON PARK » Abraham Gold, Holocaust survivor, brought Elie Wiesel's memoir "Night" to life on Wednesday, April 21 as he spoke to students at the Career Academy at South Florida Community College.

Gold recounted both the horrors of the concentration camps and the kindness of strangers who helped him despite great danger in providing him with food and assistance.

"Whatever you do, make sure you don't generalize people," Gold said to the students. "That's what they did. The devil got in them, and they did terrible things. Rather than looking for the bad in people, look for the good things."

The Career Academy at SFCC hosted Gold to further the students' lessons in their social studies and English classes, where many of them are currently reading "Night."

"This was a tremendous opportunity to further our students' education," said Jennifer Westergom, lead teacher, Career Academy. "The students got to hear a true eyewitness account of this historical event. Such accounts are becoming very rare as this generation is laid to rest. We hope his speech showed our students the dangers of hatred and prejudice."

Same year I did speak to the Students Warner University
Lake Wales, FL

Above are some letters received from students of different
schools, and show a great deal of gratitude they have for me.
It encourages me to speak again in the future.

These photos were obtained by an American pilot over the Concentration Camp Auschwitz 1n 1944. The pilot gave the photos taken to his friend, Staff Sgt. Russ Hyatt, who came to my home after he read in the town newspaper I am a holocaust survivor and he presented me with the photos. The original photos were sent to the museum in Miami, FL and copies were sent to the museum in Washington DC.

THE ORIGINAL PREISLER (GOLD) FAMILY

Father: Jacob, born 1881-1944

Mother: Blanca, born 1883-1944

Son: Shlomo, born 1905-1944

Daughter Sose, born 1908-1944

Son: Leon, born 1910-

Son: Sulem, born 1913-

Son: Willy, born 1915-

Son: Fulop, born 1918-

Son: Alex, born 1921-

Daughter: Sury, born 1923-1944

Son: Martin, born 1926-1945

Son: Abraham, born 1926-

Leon   Salem   Willie

Fulop   Alex   Sury

Martin   Abraham

Sincerely

Abraham Gold